City
Apartments

City
Apartments

ANTONIO CORCUERA ARANGUIZ

monsa
publications

CITY APARTMENTS
Copyright © 2005 Instituto Monsa de Ediciones, S.A

Director: Josep Mª Minguet

Monsa's art director: Louis Bou

Project: Equipo Loft Publications

Editor and text: Antonio Corcuera Aranguiz

Design: Emma Termes

©INSTITUTO MONSA DE EDICIONES, S.A
Gravina 43
08930 Sant Adrià de Besòs
Barcelona
España
Tlf. + 34 93 381 00 50
Fax + 34 93 381 00 93
www.monsa.com
monsa@monsa.com

ISBN 84-96429-26-1
D.L B-27.489-2.005

Printed in Spain by Industrias Gráficas Mármol, S.L

Intro

The history of cities is the history of civilisation. Since the mechanisation of agriculture and the resulting migratory flows converted the city into the paradigm of modern society in the middle of the 19th century, the apartment has come to be the most fundamental urban residence. Throughout the last century we have seen that, in general terms, the population density and the scarcity of land have considerably reduced the size of the apartments and increased that of the buildings. Nowadays the property development bubble has forced people to move out to the industrial peripheries, and the increasingly fragmented family structure and new lifestyles –together with the inevitable demand for individual homes– has intensified the need for smaller and more flexible living accommodation.

In architectural terms, housing is a struggle between the innovation and expression demanded by the designer and the economic efficacy and continuity to which the promoter and the city aspire, protagonists of a process which, on occasions, exclude the occupant, who in turn seeks a home with which he can identify. Within a programme which generally is restricted –bedrooms, lounges, bathrooms and kitchens–, the architectural solutions are adapted out of necessity to maximise the available spaces, improve the illumination and above all, endow the home with atmosphere. In effect, since the intrinsic uniformity of the apartment, the most individuality possible has been sought.

This selection of collective housing projects covers a wide range of possibilities within its category, in such a way that equally included are government protected housing projects –simple apartment blocks of which the entire architectural exercise is concentrated on the facades and interior distribution– as luxury apartments which constitute an alternative to the house. From small blocks up to large housing developments, including refurbishments and eminently vertical constructions, all the projects are innovative housing proposals, the objective of which is to apportion quality of life. Indispensable factors with regard to housing conceptions are the continuity and improvement of housing types; an awareness of environmental factors and the use of locally available materials; the constructive and collective examination of urban facades and, above all, the introduction of variety in the accommodation thanks to combined design programmes. The multi purpose buildings, which incorporate housing, offices, shops and even small hotels, reflect the eclectic reality of the contemporary city.

To establish some degree of order within the great diversity of housing presented, the projects are in order of size, from the smallest to the largest. This order facilitates a gradual interpretation and establishes links and differences in so far as the blocks expand until finally becoming, metaphorically speaking, miniature cities.

Apartments in Schaerbeek

MARIO GARZANITI

The city of Brussels is somewhat reticent towards contemporary architecture, perhaps on account of the radical historicist inflexibility. Fortunately, there are incentives, in this case public, which encourage the development of simple yet eloquent projects.

A prime example is this small building, set on the corner of a block which looks onto a plaza with an incessant flow of people. A plain and simple construction, covered with a single material: oxidised steel cut in 4mm thick panels. This apparently formal simplicity, in reality hides architecture with little in the way of detail. To avoid a mundane symmetry on the façade, each steel panel has been oxidised in a distinct manner, creating a subtle mosaic of assorted hues. The outcome is a structure resembling an untreated block of metal which has been sculpted and hollowed out to be made habitable. An industrial metaphor, the cavities of which symbolize its agenda: a street level shop and two simple but comfortable 80m^2 and 100m^2 duplexes.

Location: Brussels, Belgium I **Date of construction:** 2003 I **Surface area:** 325 m^2 I **Photography:** Alain Janssens

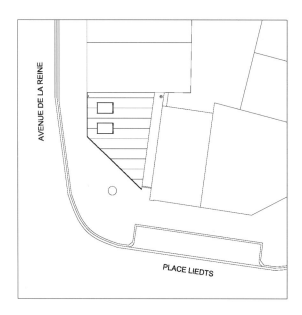

Site plan

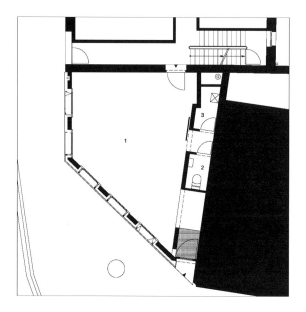

Commercial ground floor

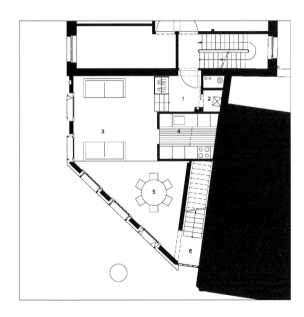

First floor

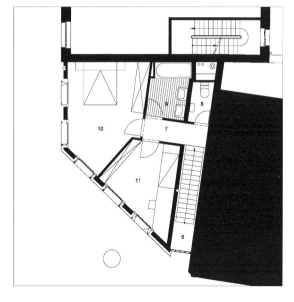

Second floor

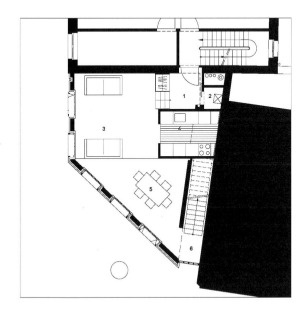

Third floor

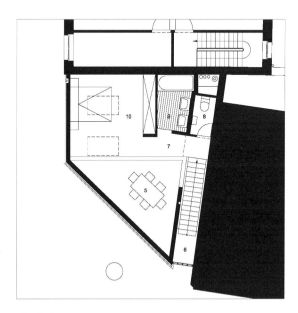

Fourth floor

0   1   2

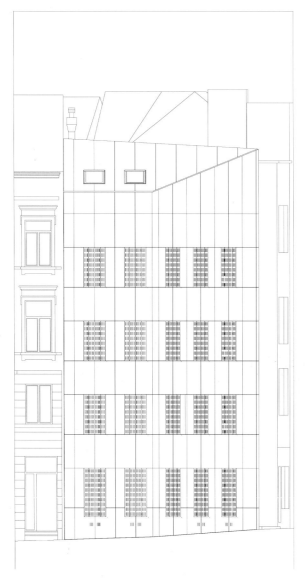

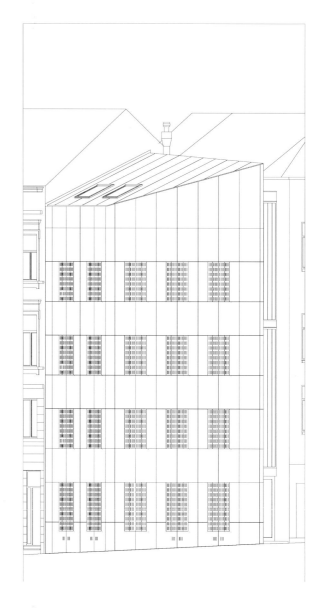

Elevations

The cut panels are emphasized by omega steel profiles and sealed with polyurethane. The blinds, likewise, create a perfect continuity on the façade and increase the block's physical presence.

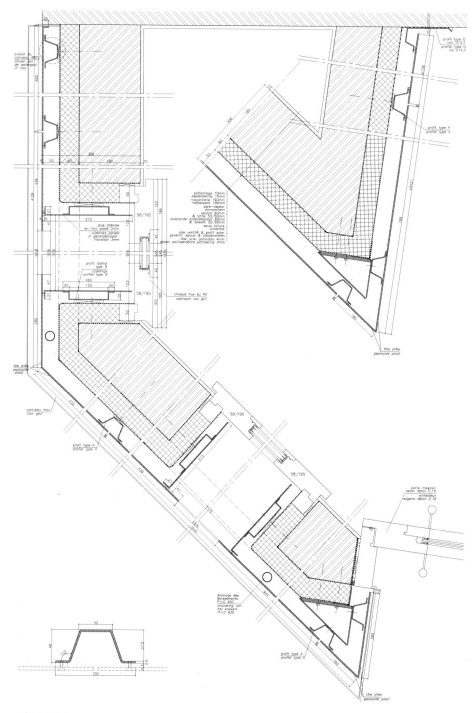

Plan details

Circus & Circus

NORISADA MAEDA/N MAEDA ATELIER

In a highly developed technological and industrial zone on the outskirts of Tokyo, this project houses apartments for eight families on a very long narrow plot located in a district with a height restriction of five floors.

To avoid a markedly linear outline, the building has been designed around curved walls: four "waves" 18m long which completely transform the concept of space and create an ambiguous and dynamic ambience. The sinuous curves translate into an interior landscape in permanent motion, further enhanced by the sober white painted finishes and polished surfaces. The apartments are narrow volumes which occupy the full depth of the building, with neither separations nor dividing walls to break the spatial continuity. Three apertures have been integrated next to the interior curves which apportion light from above and ventilation to the four storeys. These light apertures, positioned next to the small terraces on the south-facing façade of each floor, help to increase the presence of outside in the apartments.

Location: Ushiku, Japan I **Date of construction:** 2004 I **Surface area:** 412 m² I **Photography:** Nacása & Partners

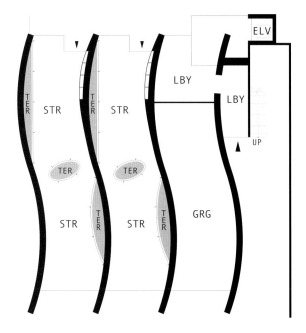

Ground floor

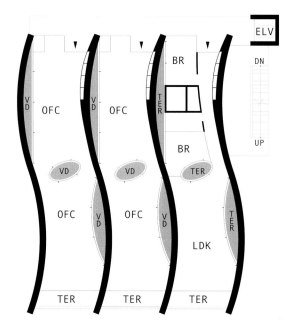

First floor

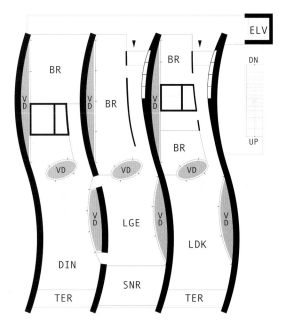

Second floor

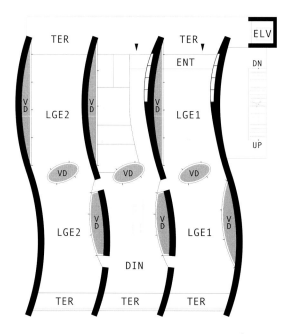

Third floor

0 1 2

G40

INNOCAD

Apartments for students and young families require, on the one hand, particular solutions with regard to the organisation of the accommodation and, on the other hand, creative implementation within a historic urban context. This refurbishment project retains its main façade, that of a typical Biedermeier house and proposes a new colourful rear façade, reflecting the building's contemporary use.

The building has been internally renovated to house four apartments of some 80m^2 and three studios of 40m^2, together with community areas and basic facilities which maximise the available space. The interiors combine materials such as polycarbonate panels, sliding lacquered doors, parquet floor tiles and white cement which contrast with the original solid wooden structure. Each residence has a terrace of at least 12m^2, which considerably increases the interior space and changes the look of the building's rear façade. The terraces –protected by adjustable fabric blinds in warm shades– permit the degree of exposure to be adjusted and create a certain ambiguity between public and private space.

Location: Graz, Austria I **Date of construction:** 2002 I **Surface area:** 435 m^2 I **Photography:** Paul Ott

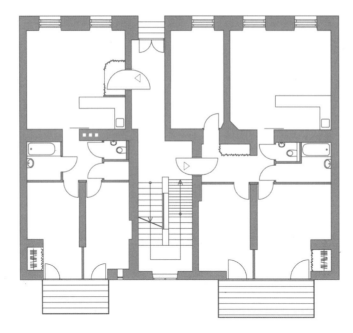

Ground floor

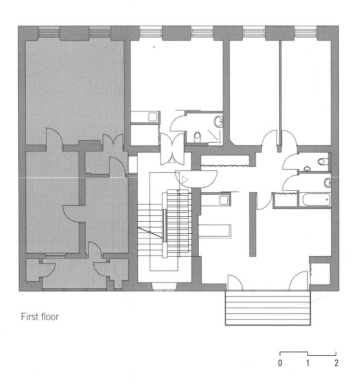

First floor

0 1 2

The project respects the original classic facade and structure, having developed the rear section of the building in order to preserve the magnitude and style of its historic context.

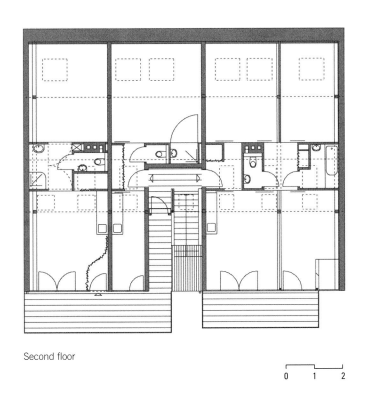

Second floor

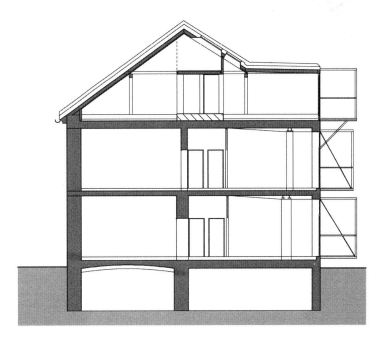

Longitudinal section

0   1   2

Elevations

Mulackstrasse 12

ABCARIUS & BURNS ARCHITECTURE DESIGN

This building, located in the historic centre of Berlin, offers an urban way of life in which flexibility and functionality determine the space therein, and which produce a permanent ambiguity between what is public and what is private.

Formally, the glazed façade on to the street seeks to reflect the scale and profundity of the neighbouring constructions, whilst the rooftop apartment, set back from the main façade, is a reinterpretation of the habitual ridged roof. An array of latticed aluminium windows define the exterior and enable the level of exposure through the large floor to ceiling windows to be regulated. The homes are of a similar layout which channel the light towards the interior and incorporate mobile walls and doors to freely transform the spaces. On the other hand, thanks to the materials used –limestone, walnut and white paint– the available natural light has been maximised to the full. Each one of the apartments has a generous exterior space in the form of a patio or terrace which strengthens the organic nature of these homes and provides a contrast with the urban environment in which they are found.

Location: Berlin, Germany | **Date of construction:** 2004 | **Surface area:** 610 m² | **Photography:** Hisao Suzuki

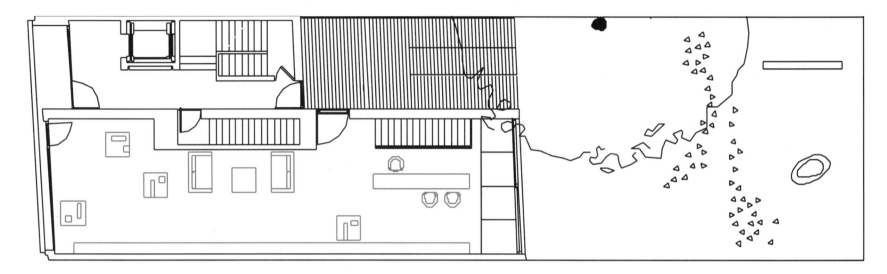

Ground floor

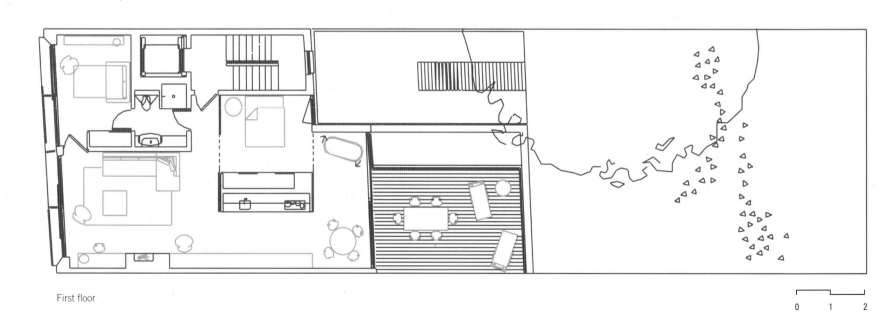

First floor

0   1   2

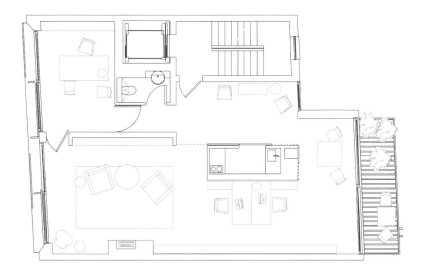

Second floor

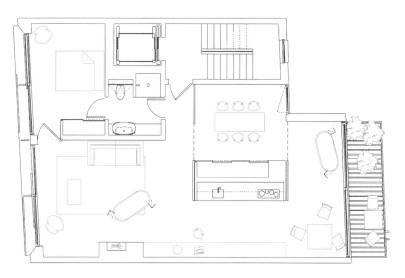

Third floor

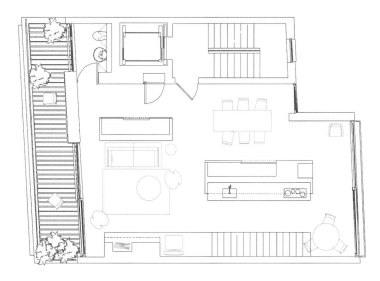

Lower level of rooftop apartment

Upper level of rooftop apartment

0   1   2

Clydebank Apartments

BBP ARCHITECTS

Located on the privileged sea front promenade alongside the city's port, the aim of this project was to transform a three storey block into three spacious apartments.

The building –originally constructed in the seventies for the purpose of a chemical laboratory– was renovated on the interior to house four garages with living accommodation above. Originally being an industrial construction with spacious areas, the refurbishment project centred on providing the necessary equipment and décor for living accommodation. The main intervention was carried out on top of the existing block: two additional storeys which house a large duplex loft with a terrace and swimming pool. The extension is designed principally of steel and glass, with contrasting colours and a light metallic structure which delicately covers the building. By means of small insets, balconies and a selection of windows, this framework creates an external sheath with the capacity to transform and bestow dynamism upon this eminently two-dimensional façade.

Location: Melbourne, Australia I **Date of construction:** 2000 I **Surface area:** 720 m² I **Photography:** Chris Ott

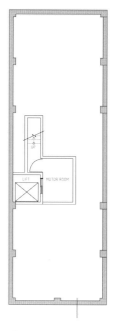

Basement

Ground floor

First floor

Second floor

Third floor

Fourth floor

0   1   2

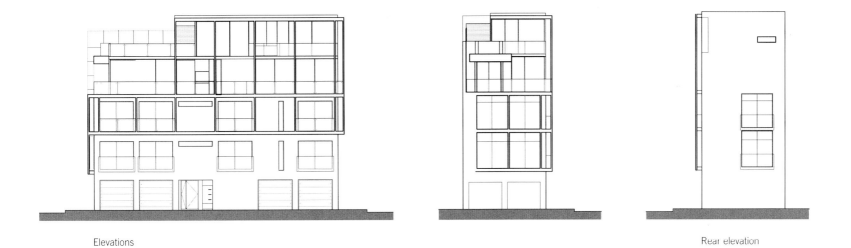

Elevations

Rear elevation

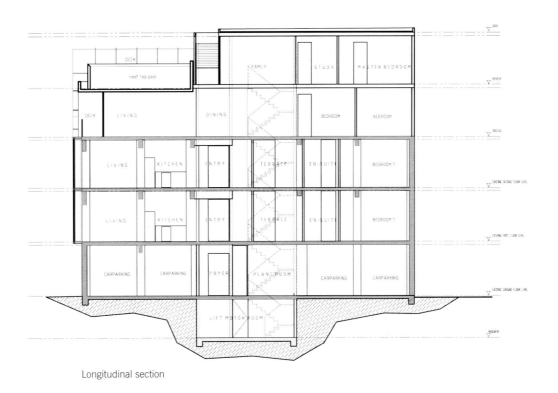

Longitudinal section

Split

CHIBA MANABU ARCHITECTS

In an area in which building plots represent a ratio of fifty percent developed-vacant with many alleyways, gardens and private patios, this project plans to construct two independent blocks united by a completely open patio.

The main block consists of eight small duplex apartments for letting, whilst the smaller building is the home of the project developer and owner. To maintain the apparent height restrictions of the buildings in the district, the top floor of both blocks has been set back from the street. The paths and staircases providing access to the homes are all external, allowing the best use to be made of the available surface area. Preserving the scale and emphasising the relationship between construction and patio space is the fundamental principal behind this project, to the extent that all the windows –likewise the spaces in general– have been designed with the purpose of creating a visual interrelation with this element. Being completely dedicated to the outside, the accommodation therefore instils a great feeling of space and amplitude albeit within a scant 60m².

Location: Tokyo, Japan I **Date of construction:** 2002 I **Surface area:** 494 m² + 175 m² I **Photography:** Nacása & Partners

To be able to preserve the scale and permitted construction density in the district, the project consists of two independent buildings united by means of a communal patio which creates a large open space between the blocks.

Ground floor

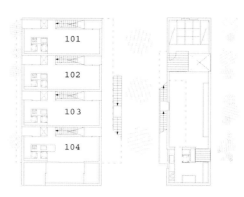

First floor

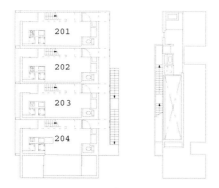

Second floor

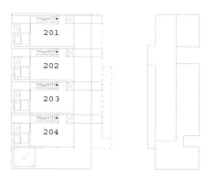

Third floor

0 2 4

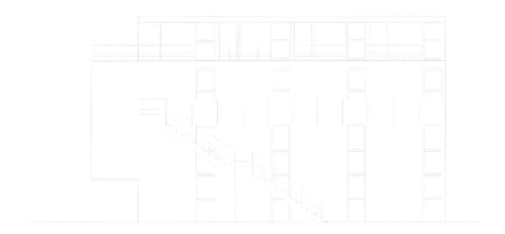

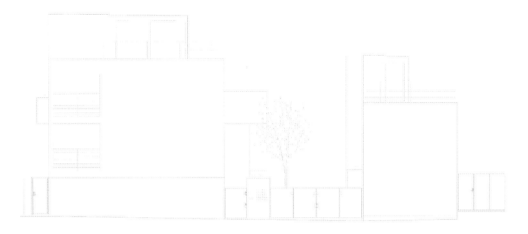

Elevations

Slender-Bender

DEADLINE

In what was to be their first major project, the architects adopted the role of designers and promoters to maximise the creative potential of this project, the site of which was a narrow plot with an old building located at the back.

The project, executed in two phases, is a complex amalgamation between the new construction and the renovation of the existing building. The intention being to create a new urban typology with a mixed appeal: the combined property houses a large apartment over three levels, a shop at street level, mini-lofts, studios and offices. The spaces have been designed to offer maximum flexibility, in such a way that the 45m² mini-lofts can serve as either homes, alternatives to hotels or small offices. Externally, the new edifice embraces the old with its essentially curved steel and glass structure projected horizontally towards the street. The aluminium sheets on the façade reflect the district's most predominant hues at the same time allowing the building to be integrated within the urban context, in spite of its strong contemporary accent.

Location: Berlin, Germany | **Date of construction:** 2002-2004 | **Surface area:** 840 m² | **Photography:** Ludger Paffrath

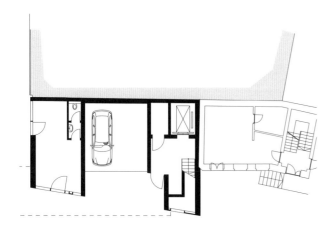

Ground floor

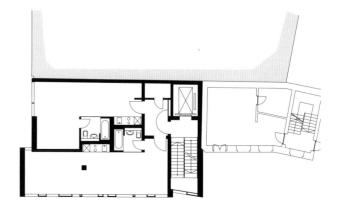

Floor plan

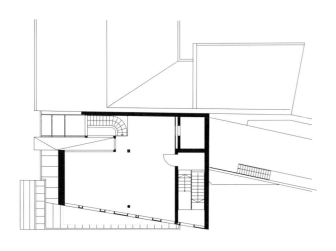

Fifth floor

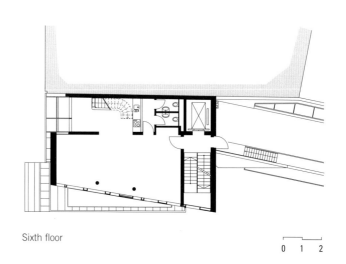

Sixth floor

0   1   2

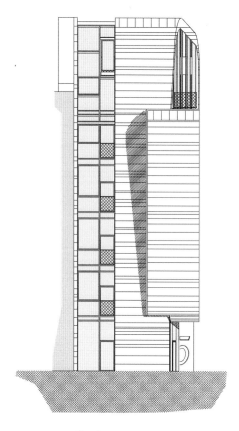

Elevation

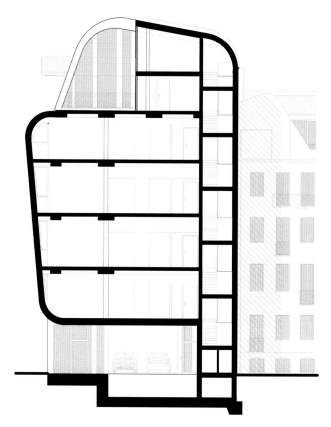

Longitudinal section

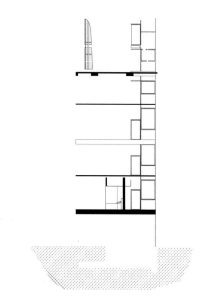

Transversal section

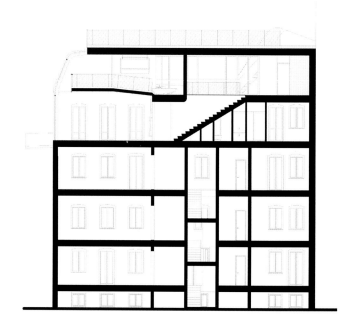

Longitudinal section

Lofts in Gràcia

JUAN TRIAS DE BES/TDB ARQUITECTURA

This project consists of transforming some pharmaceutical laboratories, constructed at the end of the fifties, into loft type living accommodation. The intervention began with a clearing operation next to the dividing wall to acquire the room to move and provide ventilation, which was to reveal the original structure of the building. With a strong industrial accent, this steel skeleton –illuminated from above– adopted the leading role in creating a dialogue with the brickwork of the dividing wall.

The loft apartments are designed with a single compact service nucleus around which the occupants can decide the manner in which the rooms are to be used and organized. This concept liberates space, permitting the creation of open and variable distributions or, alternatively, the introduction of wall partitions for a traditional apartment layout. In this respect, the lack of constructed surface area is fully compensated by the improved quality and flexibility of the residences. The ground floor is also set aside for living accommodation, with plans to re-establish the characteristics typical of the houses in Gràcia.

Location: Barcelona, Spain I **Associates:** Jordi Parramón, Justin Baroncea I **Date of construction:** 2003 I **Surface area:** 1.274 m² I **Photography:** Alejo Bagué

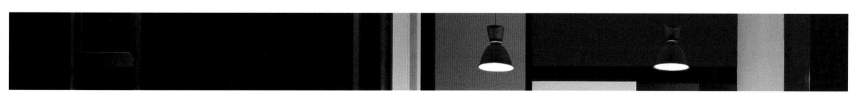

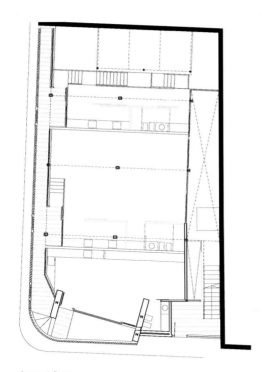

Ground floor

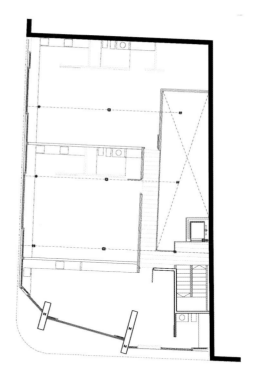

Floor plan

0   1   2

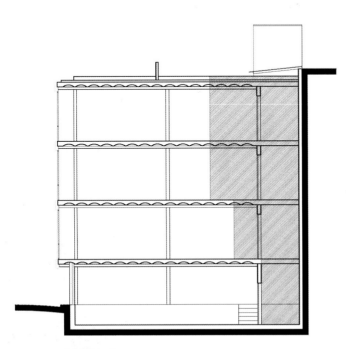

Original section

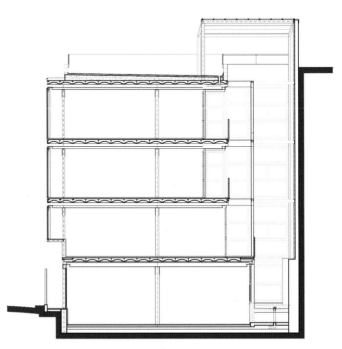

Resultant section

18 Lansdowne Crescent

JOHN PAWSON

Located in one of the most exclusive parts of the city, the simplicity and exacting symmetry of this building, designed by John Pawson, stands out amongst the classic mansions in this district.

The building is a restrained white stone mass, almost devoid of constructional elements with huge six meter high windows facing on to the crescent. The interior layout, designed by Paul Davis, conveys the exterior simplicity to the most open distribution possible, with luxurious double height spaces, three bedrooms, two bathrooms and a kitchen. A long way from the conventional idea of an apartment block, with five lateral units distributed over complete floors with the approximate surface area of a typical London terraced house. The residences therefore combine the character and privacy of a family house with the security and convenience associated with an apartment. The overall result is a building which demonstrates the ability to respond to the classic expression of a district such as Notting Hill with a contemporary, elegant and at the same time simple design.

Location: London, United Kingdom I **Associates:** Paul Davis & Partners (interiors) I **Date of project:** 2004 I **Surface area:** 1.300 m² I **Photography:** Adam Parker

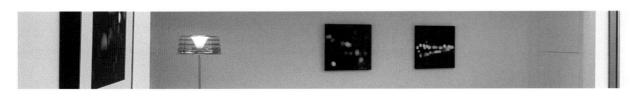

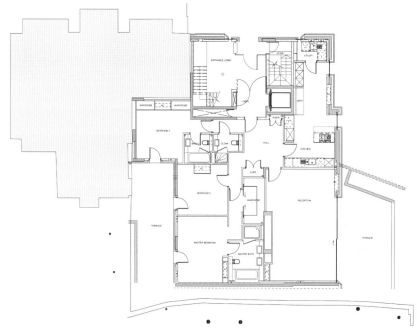

Ground floor

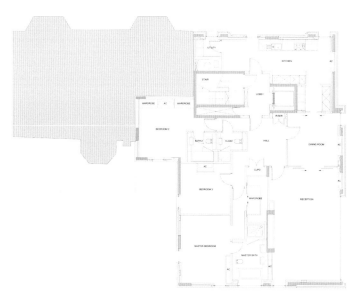

First floor

The building, with its simple facades, provides a dialogue between the two settings, on the one hand the grand Victorian mansions on Lansdowne Crescent, and the adjacent blocks on the other.

0   1   2

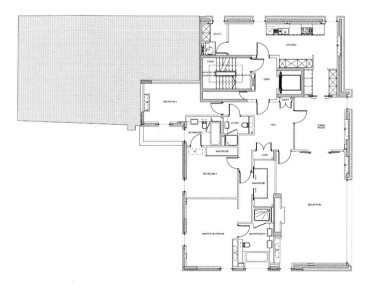

Second floor

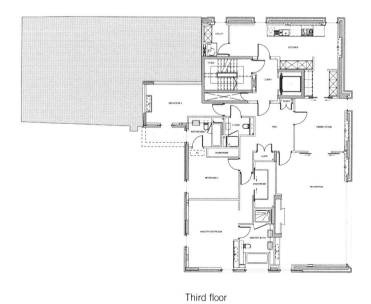

Third floor

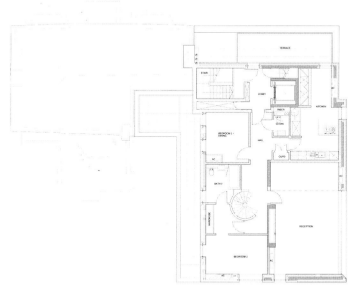

Fourth floor

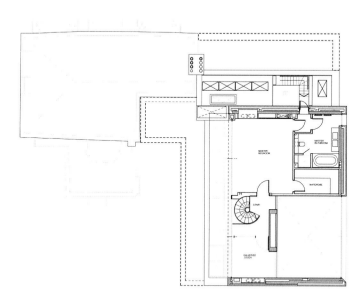

Fifth floor

0   1   2

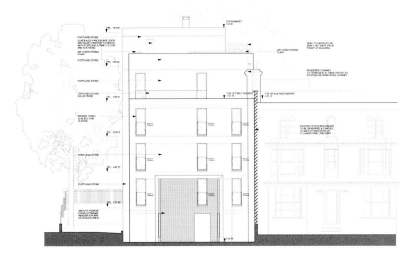

North elevation

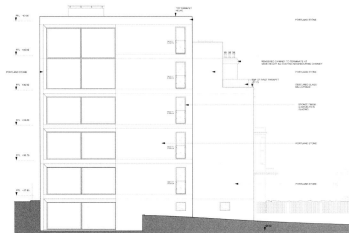

East elevation

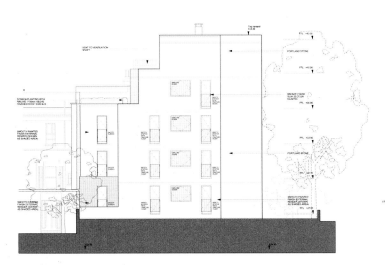

South elevation

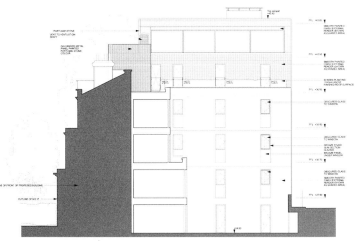

West elevation

1310 East Union

MILLER HULL PARTNERSHIP

This building, situated on a small plot surrounded by buildings on three sides, has been developed vertically up to the permitted height limit to accommodate eight lofts of between 65 and 150 m².

The construction solution was easily established: a glass box with a steel skeleton over seven levels between party walls. This Meccano type structure –enabled the building to be raised rapidly and simply– giving the structure as a whole a visually light and transparent appearance amongst a background of lower buildings. With a north south orientation, the completely glazed façades maximise natural light and maintain a connection with the outside, a vital aspect for the city's inhabitants. The floors are completely open, with prefabricated concrete blocks covered with undulating steel and an abundance of metallic finishes giving the interior an industrial and highly functional appearance. The building represents a well chosen design with an efficient and simple structural appearance, essential characteristics for the lifestyle associated with an urban loft.

Location: Seattle, United States I **Date of construction:** 2001 I **Surface area:** 1.560 m² I **Photography:** James Housel

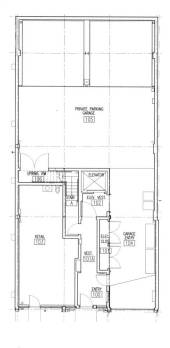

Ground floor

First floor

Second floor

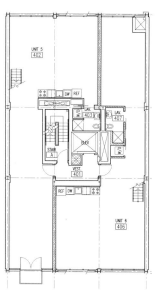

Third floor

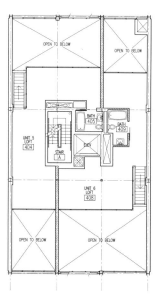

Third floor loft

Fourth floor

Attic

0 1 2

Axonometric section

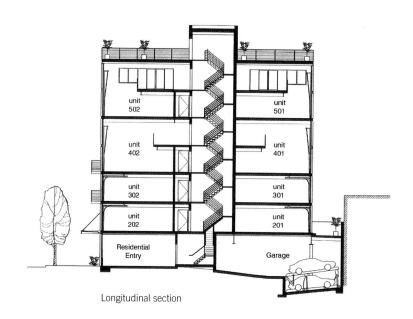

unit 502
unit 402
unit 302
unit 202
Residential Entry

unit 501
unit 401
unit 301
unit 201
Garage

Longitudinal section

The top floors house two duplexes, both 150m² with private south facing balconies and with a communal hanging garden on the roof terrace.

AR 58

DEREK DELLEKAMP/DELLEKAMP ARQUITECTOS

In this project located on one of the borders of Colonia Condesa, the southerly orientation became the departure point from which to create an interior north facing patio, around which the services are gathered. Each level responds to a specific situation with respect to the exterior –open onto the tree tops, closed to the noisy avenue, completely open on the top floor– depending on the height at which it is found. As a result, the distribution of each apartment is different, creating homes which are easily identifiable as distinct units, reflecting their future occupants. From the outside they appear to be large boxes or containers, with a smooth, undulating aluminium skin with a white and naturally anodized finish. These four finishes react differently to the light and create a dynamic and ever changing façade. To separate the residences from the vehicular comings and goings on the street, these are allocated as from the second floor up; the former levels designated to facilities for the whole building: parking, access and business premises.

Location: Mexico DF, Mexico I Date of construction: 2003 I Surface area: 2.009 m² I Photography: Oscar Necoechea, Lara Becerra

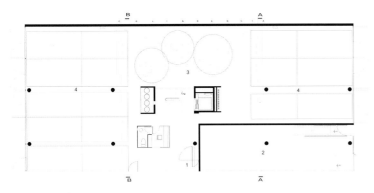

Ground floor

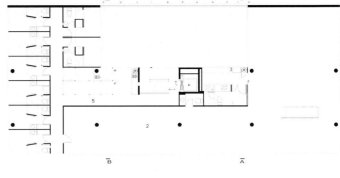

First floor

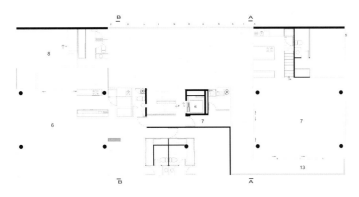

Second floor

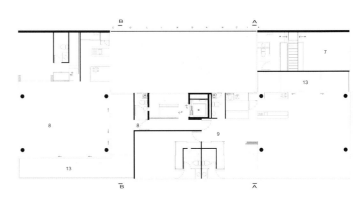

Third floor

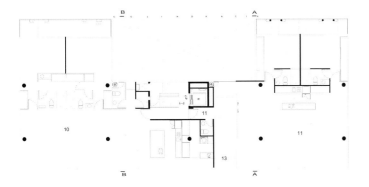

Fourth floor

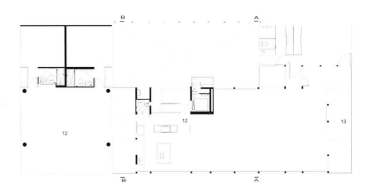

Fifth floor

0   1   2

South elevation

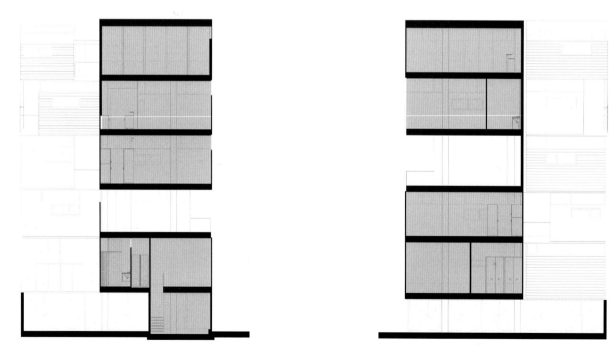

Transversal sections

Edificio Parque España

TEN ARQUITECTOS

This seven story building, situated on a corner opposite the park of the same name, houses six large apartments with a modern art gallcry and parking on the ground floor.

As each apartment occupies an entire floor, they are set out like open plan lofts in which the future occupants can design and fit out the rooms according to their needs and desires. The bedrooms are generally orientated towards the street and are protected by a narrow balcony with an aluminium structure. This framework, dressed with translucent acrylic sliding doors, is the most characteristic element of the building, providing the apartments with both privacy and filtered light. The floors are further extended in a southerly direction by ledged balconies open to views of the park.

The apartments are accessed by means of a bridge united to the lateral service area –next to the rear façade– which contains the main staircase, whilst a second spiral staircase leads to the magnificent rooftop terrace with pool.

Location: Mexico DF, Mexico I **Date of construction:** 2001 I **Surface area:** 2.200 m² I **Photography:** Jaime Navarro

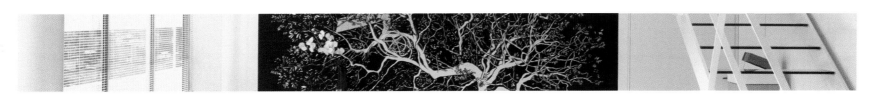

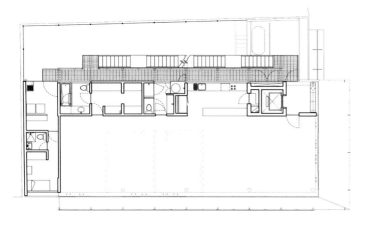

Floor type

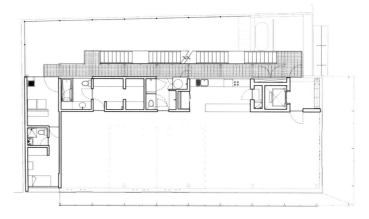

Lower level of the attic apartment

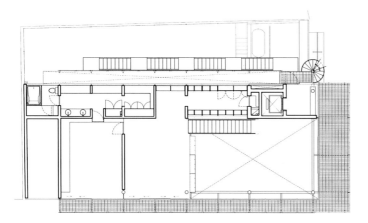

Upper level of attic apartment

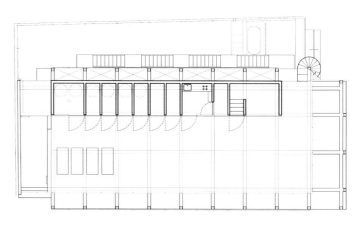

Terrace

0   2   4

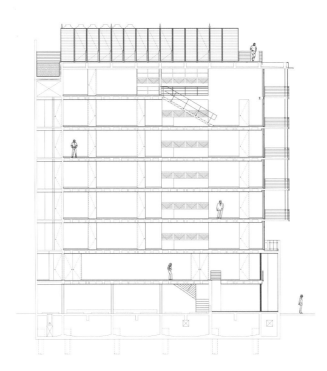

Longitudinal section

Balmes 145

ESTUDIO CARLOS FERRATER

Located on a typical city plot between party walls, this 11.60m wide building represents a clever interpretation of Barcelona's housing regulations.

The project has been developed with three levels destined to a commercial establishment, four to residences –two to each landing– and three to underground parking. In keeping with the regulations, the façade is structured around vertical elements with fifty percent covered-empty made up of both fixed and mobile pieces, giving the building a visually dynamic appearance. In effect, the façade is made up of four layers, the total thickness of which amounts to 40cm: an interior pane of glass, sliding wooden screen, steel grill and a silver quartzite roller blind. This provides the apartments with varying degrees of illumination and exposure to the outside, which filters both light and street noise. The huge ground floor apertures onto the street present an urban vision of transparency and maintain a certain ambiguity between the interior and the exterior.

Location: Barcelona, Spain I **Associates:** Joan Guibernau, Lucía Ferrater I **Date of construction:** 2002 I **Surface area:** 2.750 m² I **Photography:** Alejo Bagué

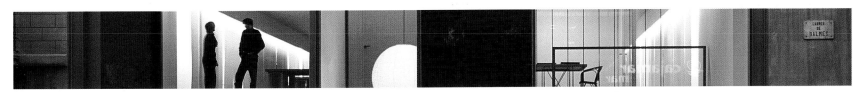

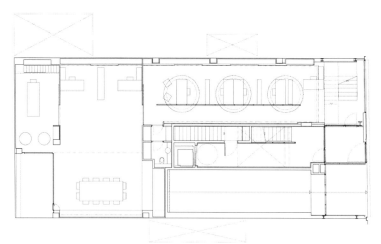

Ground floor of commercial establishment

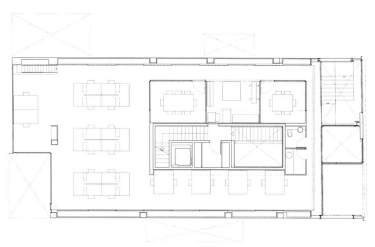

Loft of commercial establishment

Floor plan

0 1 2

Elevation

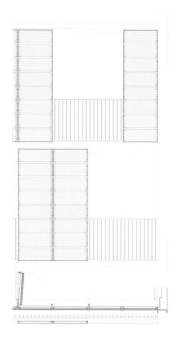

Latticed window detail

Homes on Carré Mainzer Landstrasse

BRT ARCHITEKTEN

This Project is an example of the current urban transformations taking place in European cities, a process by which the old industrial zones are restructured to create a valuable multi purpose development. More specifically, this housing plan forms part of an important complex close to Frankfurt's financial district, which conceptually presents a gradual transition between the district's old residential buildings and the adjacent office blocks.

The building's interior is organised around two stairwells located next to the principal façade and which serve as an entrance hall, since the ground floor is also living accommodation. The accommodation is distributed over two L shaped levels, which negates the need for distribution corridors and make full use of the upper level of the two. The layout of the apartments permits an influential feature to be created thanks to the windows and balconies being arranged on the rear façade, looking out onto a large garden which creates a green breathing space amongst the buildings.

Location: Frankfurt, Germany I **Date of construction:** 2003 I **Surface area:** 3.800 m² I **Photography:** Jörg Hempel

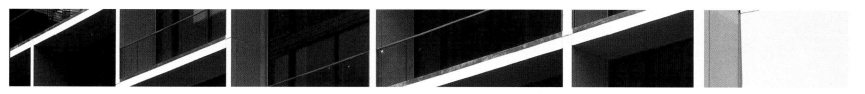

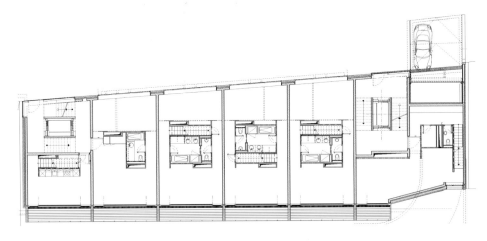

Ground floor

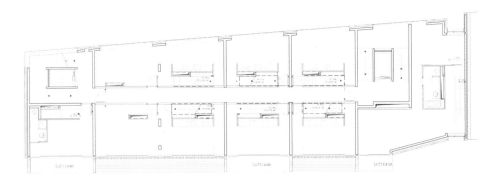

Lower level type

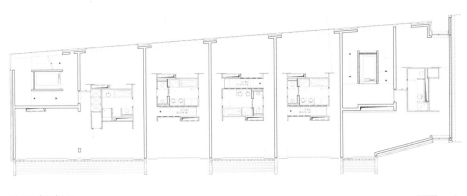

Upper level type

0   1   2

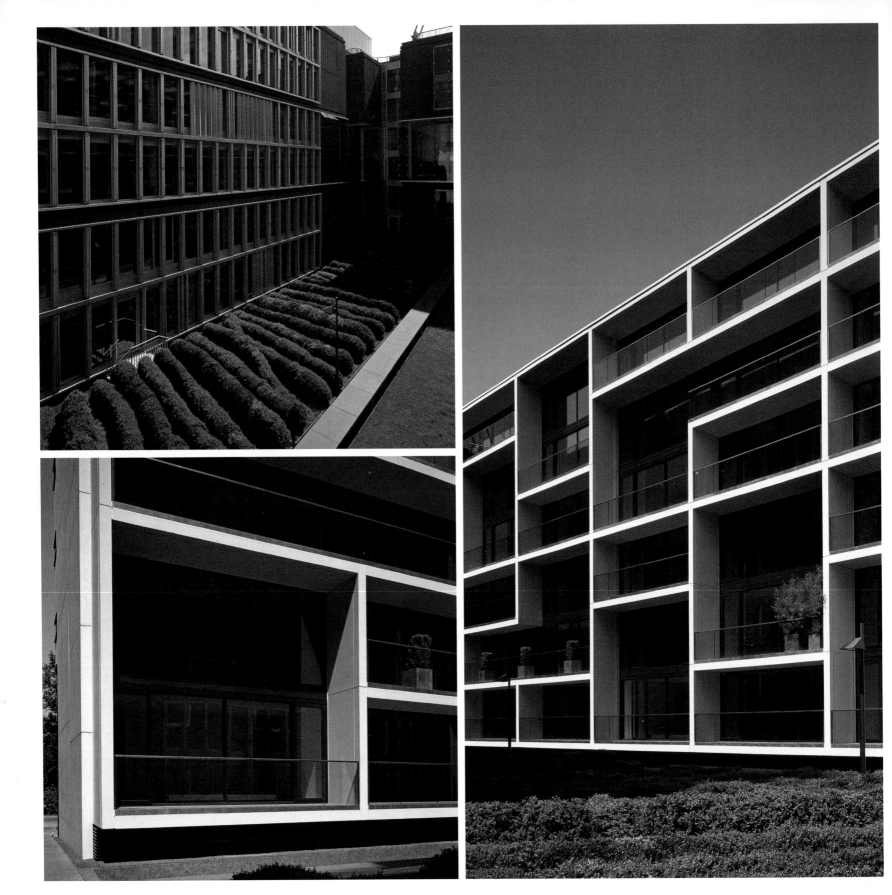

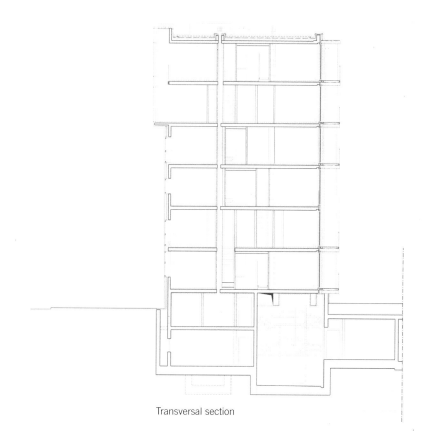

Transversal section

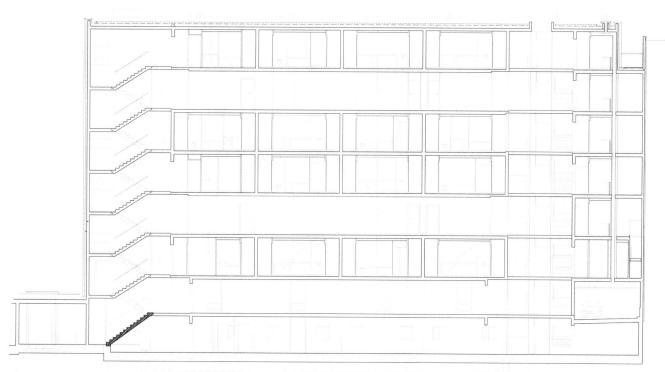

Longitudinal section

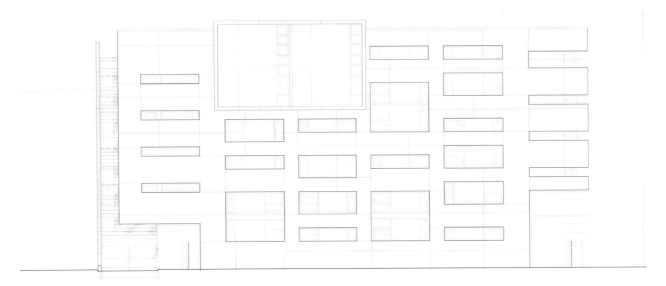

Front elevation

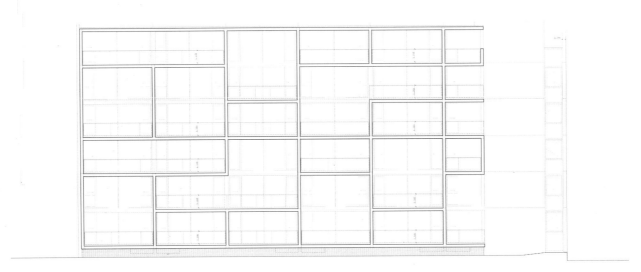

Rear elevation

The residences are distributed
over two L shaped floors,
of ample and functional
proportions around a service
nucleus.

Hermosilla 18

VICENS & RAMOS

To construct a building with living accommodation in a completely established district means having to abide by regulations which limit the design but which also help to maintain certain architectural values typical to the city.

The intention behind this project was not only to respect the pre-existing but also to reinforce it apportioning contemporary qualities. The granite covered building is therefore arranged in three sections maintaining the classic layout: basement with commercial space on the first two floors, the intermediate zone for living accommodation with a façade without decorative elements and a varied height rooftop loft apartment with a topping on the corner reminiscent of traditional fortified towers. To counteract the eminently vertical development, the recess lintels join to form small eaves per floor which reproduce the projection of the large canopy above the attic. This composition respects the buildings around it, and by substituting the traditional decoration with functional and quality construction, it provides a harmony between past and present.

Location: Madrid, Spain | **Associate:** Carlos Bringas | **Date of construction:** 2004 | **Surface area:** 4.600 m² | **Photography:** Eugeni Pons

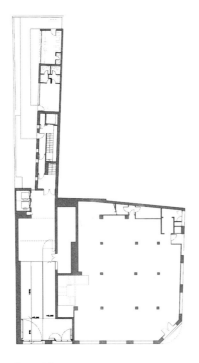

Ground floor

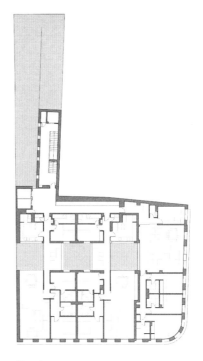

Floor type

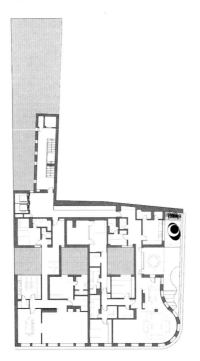

Lower level of the loft apartment

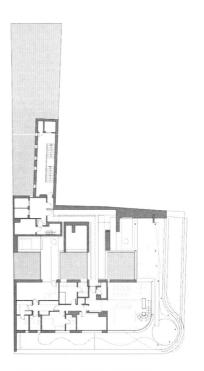

Upper level of the loft apartment

0   2   4

The building is topped on the corner by a loft of variable height, a reinterpretation of the towers which used to crown the stately buildings of old.

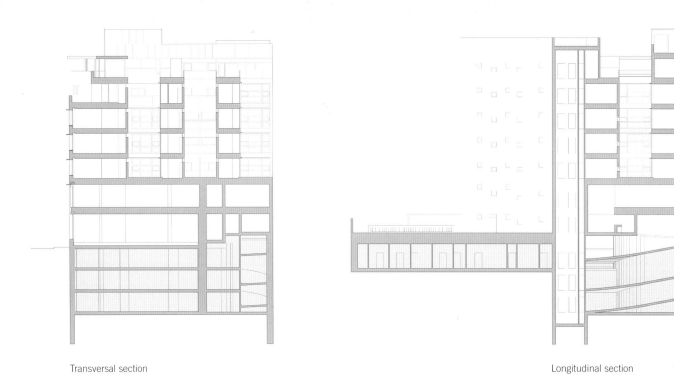

Transversal section   Longitudinal section

Porterhouse Apartments

SHOP – SHARPLES, HOLDEN, PASQUARELLI

Located in one of Manhattan's most vibrant districts, this project consists of converting a huge six storey warehouse into a residential building. The intervention also proposed four additional floors, projecting out in a southerly direction, with a total of 22 apartments of between 83m^2 and 315m^2.

The most interesting aspect is, without doubt, the façade to the extension, made up of a system of computer designed zinc panels with floor to ceiling windows which accentuate the building's vertical aspect. This carefully designed sheath is not structural, which apportions an exterior continuity, in spite of the differences in floor height, between the old building and the new. A numerical control process enables the panels to be accurately constructed in three sizes which are arranged in such a way as to leave spaces for the windows and light boxes, which at the same time define the interiors of the homes. The outcome is an extremely dynamic structure which creates a choreographic play on metal and glass which is illuminated by night: a new architectural milestone on Ninth Avenue.

Location: New York, United States I **Date of construction:** 2003 I **Surface area:** 4.780 m^2 I **Photography:** Seong Kwon

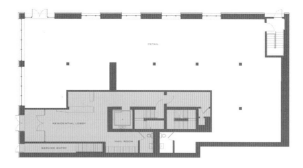

Ground floor

Floors 1-3

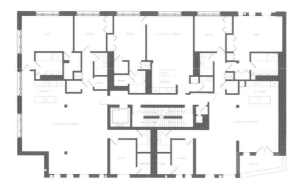

Floors 5-6

0   2   4

The building's external sheath is a
succession of zinc, glass and acrylic
panels of different widths which
provide a strong contrast against the
old brick façade.

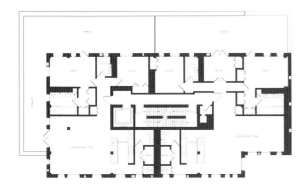

Floor 7

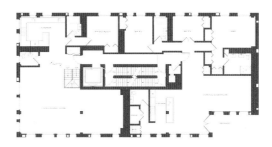

Floor 10

0   2   4

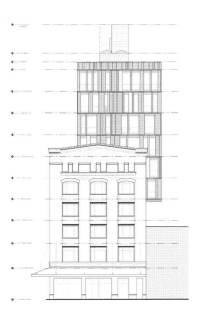

West elevation

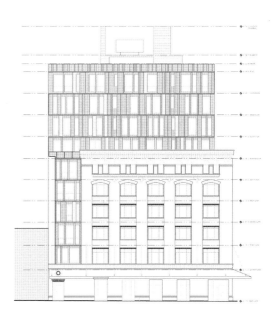

North elevation

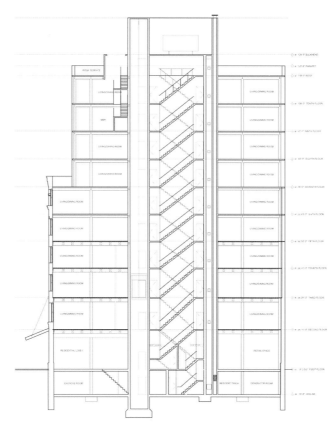

Staircase section

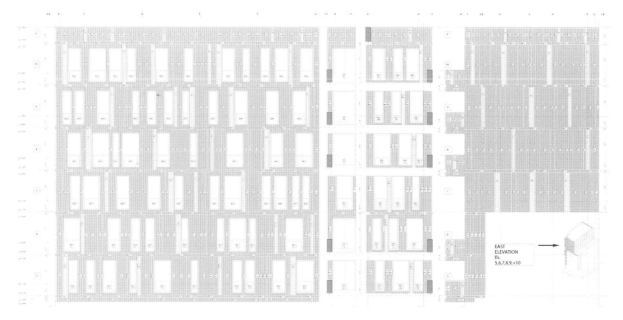

Details of the glazing on the facades

Wienerberg Lofts

DELUGAN MEISSL ASSOCIATED ARCHITECTS

This building, which forms part of the urban development of an old industrial zone in Vienna, incorporates living accommodation, offices and a nursery on the ground floor.

The architects' objectives challenge the traditional way of thinking, with units stacked one above the other, proposing a complex system of intersected levels making the accommodation complex more varied and interesting. With a predefined floor to ceiling height of 2.5m, this proposal made it possible to create sleeping zones of 2.3m and lounge areas with a 3.3m height. This innovative design, which requires numerous sections to explain its structure, permits an additional floor to be constructed on the north of the building, reserved for offices and small studios for letting purposes. The 47 apartments –from single person studios to large duplexes– are designed in the form of lofts, with the least number of divisions possible. The exterior of the building presents a noticeable contrast between its facades: on the south-facing elevation, the continuous sill of the balconies with photovoltaic panels; on the north-facing elevation, a dynamic crystal maze.

Location: Vienna, Austria | **Date of construction:** 2004 | **Surface area:** 5.313 m² | **Photography:** Hertha Hurnaus

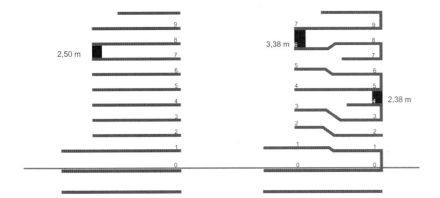

2,50 m

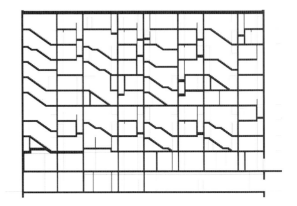

3,38 m

2,38 m

Explanation of section diagrams

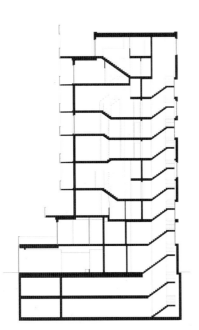

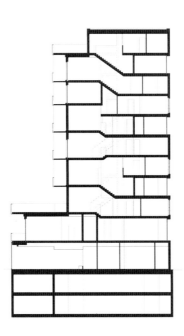

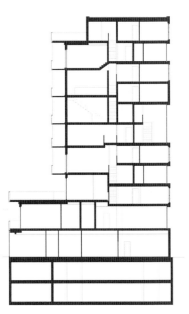

Longitudinal section

Transversal sections

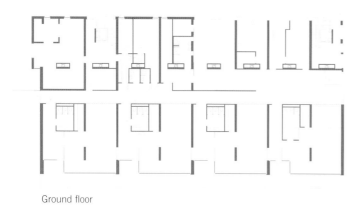

Ground floor

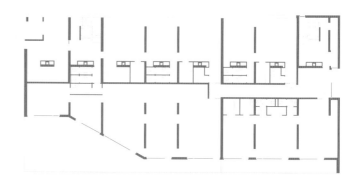

First floor

0 2 4

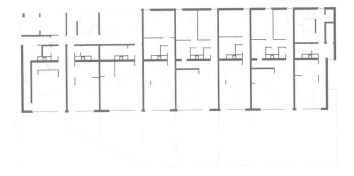

Second floor

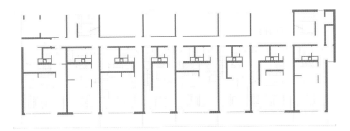

Sixth floor

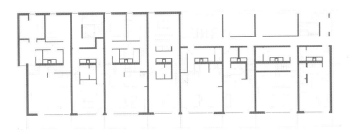

Ninth floor

0   2   4

Within the building's varied
typology, all the apartments have
spacious and continuous rooms,
dividing panels and diverse elements
being constructed in the course of
the work.

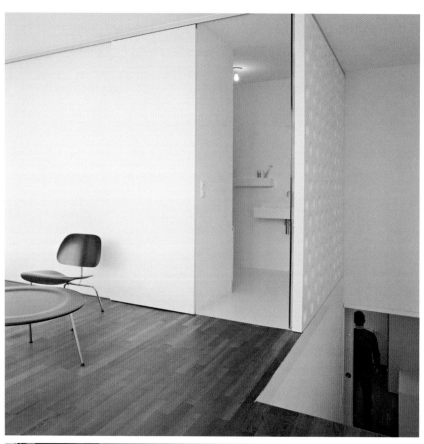
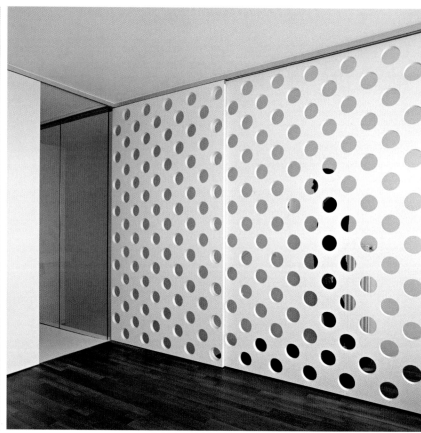

Studios for Cirque du Soleil

ÉRIC GAUTHIER/LES ARCHITECTES FABG

For approximately a decade, youngsters from every corner of the globe have converged on the famous Cirque du Soleil campus in Montreal to receive some months of instruction and training before becoming a part of the company's different spectaculars. This project provides 115 studios for these artists, as well as communal facilities, halls, offices, gymnasium, discotheque and a cybercafé.

The architectural plan basically consists of a large cube of rooms above the many facilities, joined to an adjacent accommodation building. The exterior is highlighted by metallic plaques painted in shades of copper, which react differently to light throughout the day and provide a contrast to the more vivid interior colours. The construction as a whole appears to be a collection of containers stacked high, an industrial expression which seeks to reflect the transitory nature of its occupants, together with the inevitable tensions present between the individual and collective forces of this artistic company.

Location: Montreal, Canada | **Date of construction:** 2003 | **Surface area:** 6.500 m² | **Photography:** Steve Montpetit

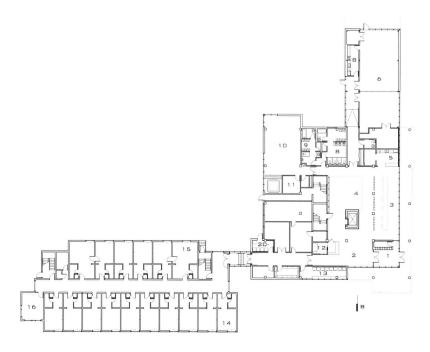

Ground floor

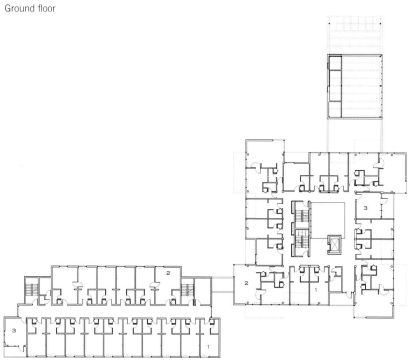

First floor

0 2 4

Second floor

Third floor

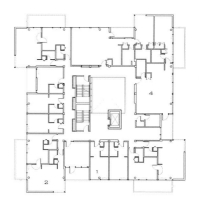

Fourth floor

0   2   4

The studios are arranged on the
interior of the cube –the colours of
which contrast with the uniformity of
the exterior– set around a great
crystal glazed void the full height of
the building.

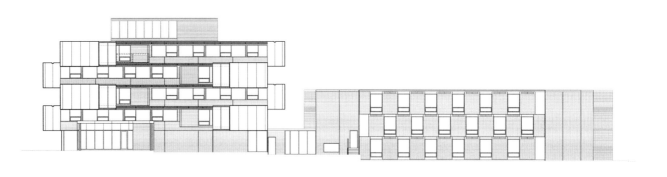

Elevations

Residences in Rafael Finat

MATOS-CASTILLO ARQUITECTOS

These homes, which abide by the construction guidelines for the district in which they are located, are the outcome of a tender, for which the architects proposed a high volume construction, divided up into three sections, with generous landscaped areas which help to dilute the density and unify the ground. Subsequently, the building had to be adapted to the norms of a seven storey confined block, although the will was preserved to create a collection of pieces above with different types of living accommodation.

As a result, the three original sections become five, a unification of independent volumes which maintain the open block concept and make full use of the plot's designated building land. Each section offers a specific configuration with regard to the type of accommodation –studios, apartments and duplexes– according to orientation and position within the block and which are distinguished by brightly coloured entrance doors on the exterior facades. The construction as a whole is united by the use of concrete and fibrocement as expressive elements, which generate a dynamic and solid composition with a great diversity of apertures and constructive elements.

Location: Barcelona, Spain | **Date of construction:** 2003 | **Surface area:** 7.418 m² | **Photography:** Hisao Suzuki

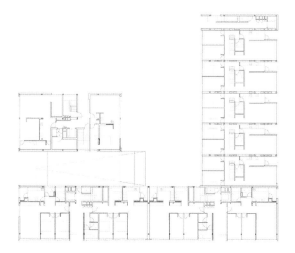

Ground floor

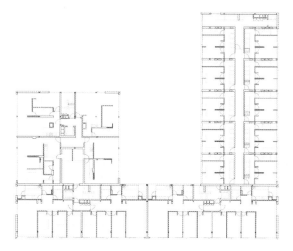

First floor

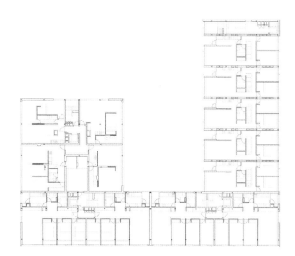

Second floor

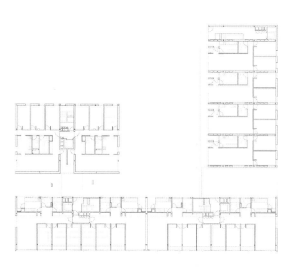

Third floor

0   2   4

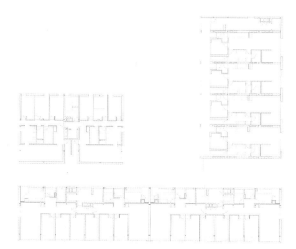

Fourth floor

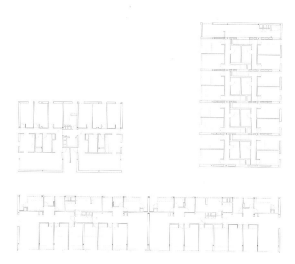

Fifth floor

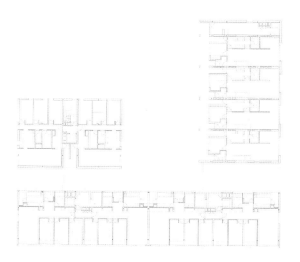

Sixth floor

0 2 4

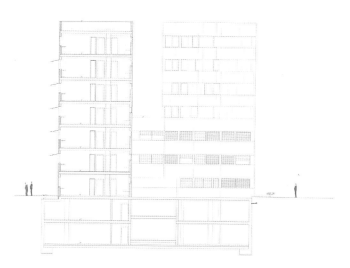

Transversal section

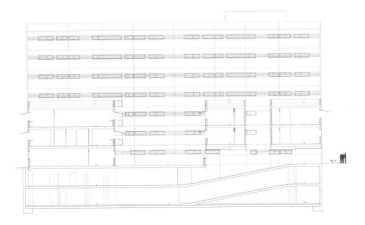

Longitudinal sections

Ter Huivra

CLAUS EN KAAN ARCHITECTEN

Ter Huivra is a building which houses 18 apartments, with offices and shops on the ground floor and parking in the basement.

The building is sculptured entirely out of the relationship established with its environment: the street, the landscape and the large park opposite, of the same name. The facades and the curved planes reduce the volumetric weight of the building to adjust to this zone's construction scale, whilst the top floor is offset in such a way that the building cannot be seen in its entirety from any angle. Consequently the block presents a fragmented image in which each curve responds differently to the incidence of the sun and the urban location. The fluidity of the glazed facades is further accentuated by the projecting terraces, which also provide the apartments with a generous exterior space and provide comfortable access to the shops and offices. The materials –steel, concrete, white painted enclosures and wood laminated terraces– are simple and help to maintain the building's strong horizontal expression.

Location: Joure, The Netherlands | **Date of construction:** 2004 | **Surface area:** 8.050 m² | **Photography:** Luuk Kramer

Site plan

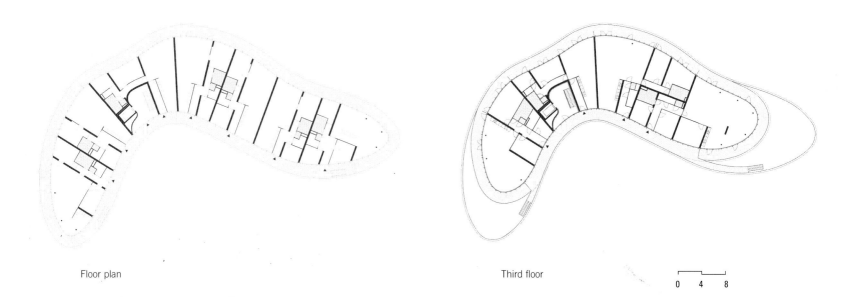

Floor plan

Third floor

0 4 8

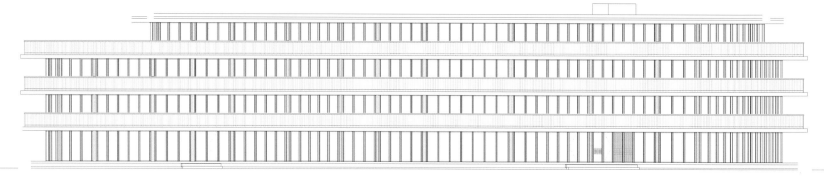

Elevation

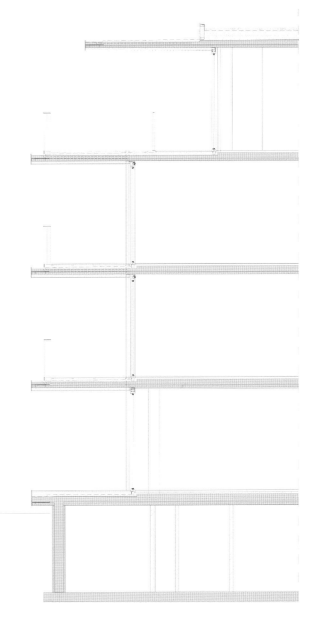

Section detail

Homes in Welserstrasse

ONE ROOM

The city of Salzburg has the good fortune of being able to offer a privileged landscape, to the extent that there are few locations in which magnificent homes cannot be constructed having made a careful study of the site. In this instance the proposal includes eight apartment blocks with generous communal gardens and a plaza in the centre of the complex.

One of the projects starting points was to provide optimum and even-handed sunlight, a fundamental aspect taking into account the city's climatic situation. As a result, the longitudinal facades of these buildings are south facing and arranged transversally in respect to the complex's central axis in order to create a volumetrically balanced distribution. The blocks themselves present slight differences, with different floor configurations, some partially protruding sections and projecting balconies which create a balance between interior and exterior. Thanks to the complex's eloquent style, photovoltaic panels and equilibrium between constructed surface area and garden space, the complex conveys a certain quality of life.

Location: Saltsburg, Austria I **Date of construction:** 2003 I **Surface area:** 9.300 m² I **Photography:** Andrew Phelps

Site plan

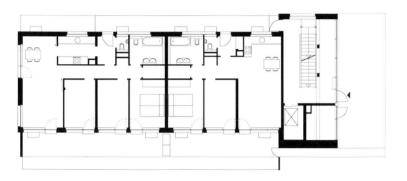

Ground floor block A

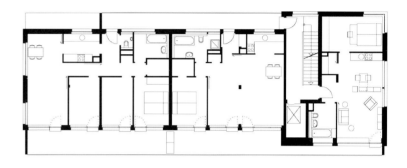

First floor block A

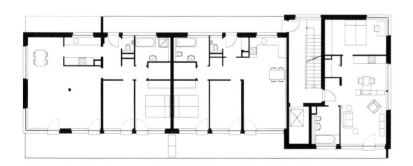

Second floor block A

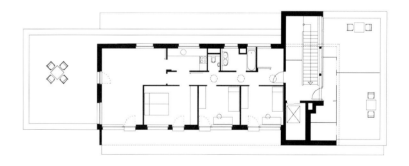

Third floor block A

0   1   2

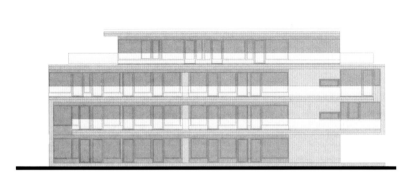

Elevation block A

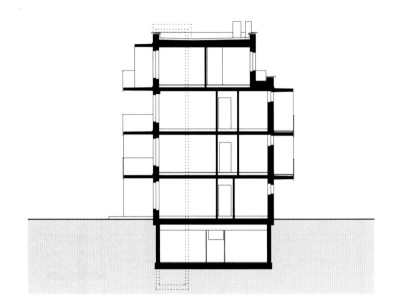

Section block A

Housing in Jerez

JOSÉ SOTO GARCÍA, FEDERICO MONTALDO MERINO

This enormous protected housing scheme is in a newly developing area in the north of Jerez, the site of which is a parcel of land left over from former promotions. The building consequently, had to be completely adapted to a long, triangular shaped plot, with open and differentiated boundaries.

The homes are distributed around entrance halls, with six apartments to each floor, three light-filled patios and a distribution nucleus. The rooms are grouped around the perimeters of the patios, through which a fully glazed gallery crosses to provide access to the homes. To avoid excessive sunlight, the building is protected from the south by a double skin, with terraces on the side which establish a continuous flow on the façade. On the north and west elevations, the apartments project outwards with ledged balconies of different sizes, creating a dynamic play on projections and recesses on the façade, whilst on the asymmetrical extremes the homes embrace the large exterior patios and interconnect by floor to complete the complex.

Location: Jerez de la Frontera, Spain I **Date of construction:** 2004 I **Surface area:** 15.931 m² I **Photography:** Fernando Alda

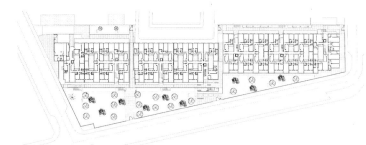

Ground floor

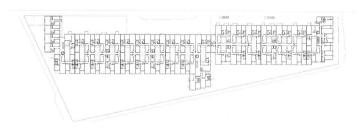

First floor

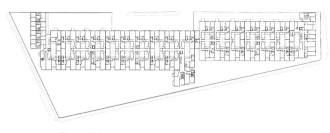

Second floor

Third floor

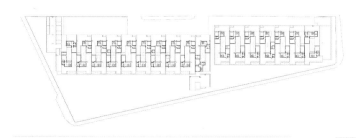

Fourth floor

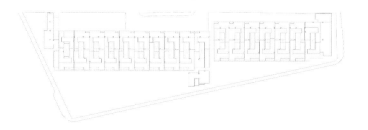

Fifth floor

0   4   8

South elevation

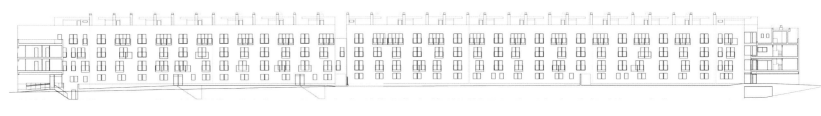

North elevation

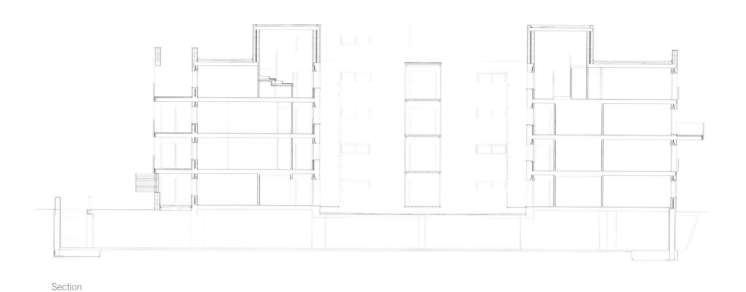

Section